THIS
BOOK
BELONGS TO

THE LIFE OF JESUS

Illustrated by Chris Molan
Written by Sally Grindley

" ... AND SHE SHALL BRING FORTH A SON, AND THOU SHALT CALL HIS NAME JESUS ... "

REVISED EDITION

DK LONDON
Senior Editor Anna Streiffert-Limerick
Senior Art Editor Rachael Grady
US Editor Jennette ElNaggar
Managing Editor Fran Baines
Managing Art Editor Phil Letsu
Production Controller Sian Cheung
Production Editor Andy Hilliard
Jacket Design Development Manager
Sophia MTT
Publisher Andrew Macintyre
Art Director Karen Self
Associate Publishing Director Liz Wheeler
Publishing Director Jonathan Metcalf

DK DELHI
Jacket Designer Juhi Sheth
DTP Designers Anurag Trivedi,
Rakesh Kumar, Vikram Singh
Senior DTP Designer Tarun Sharma
Production Manager Pankaj Sharma
Desk Editor Saumya Agarwal
Managing Editor Saloni Singh

FIRST EDITION
Project Editor Sadie Smith
Project Art Editor Polly Appleton
Managing Editor Andrew Macintyre
Managing Art Editor Jacquie Gulliver
DTP Design Siu Yin Ho
Jacket Design Dean Price
Production Jenny Jacoby

Consultant Reverend Dr. Stephen Motyer,
lecturer at the London Bible College,
London, UK.

This American Edition, 2022
First American Edition, 2003
Published in the United States
by DK Publishing
1745 Broadway, 20th Floor,
New York, NY 10019

A catalog record for this book is
available from the Library of Congress.
ISBN 978-0-7440-5026-4

DK books are available at special
discounts when purchased in bulk for
sales promotions, premiums, fund-raising,
or educational use. For details, contact:
DK Publishing Special Markets, 1745
Broadway, 20th Floor, New York, NY
10019. Special Sales@dk.com

Printed and bound in China

For the curious
www.dk.com

MIX
Paper from
responsible sources
FSC
www.fsc.org
FSC™ C018179

This book was made with Forest Stewardship
Council™ certified paper - one small step in
DK's commitment to a sustainable future.
For more information go to
www.dk.com/our-green-pledge

CONTENTS

Introduction

This is the story of Jesus, one of the most amazing people of all time. He was born more than 2,000 years ago in Bethlehem, near Jerusalem, and our years are counted from the date of his birth. Jesus's story is told in the four Gospels of the New Testament, written by Matthew, Mark, Luke, and John—four of Jesus's closest followers.

The main events of Jesus's life took place around Galilee and Judea (modern Israel and Palestine). Although he never left his home country and did not write any books, within 100 years of his death, there were groups of his followers—called Christians—all over Europe and North Africa, and as far east as India. Today, there are Christian believers in every country on Earth, and about 2 billion people—nearly one-third of the world's population—follow Jesus's teachings and worship him.

Why is this man so important? The stories that follow will tell you why. His teachings were wonderful, he could heal people of incurable illnesses, and people felt that he loved them even when no one else did. But the biggest reason for Jesus's impact comes at the end of the story—Christians believe that Jesus rose from the dead three days after his execution, and that he is alive and with us today.

"Tell the vision to no man, until the Son of Man be risen again from the dead."

MARY'S NEWS

DURING THE REIGN OF HEROD, King of Judea, a young woman named Mary lived in the town of Nazareth in Galilee. Mary was eagerly awaiting her forthcoming marriage to Joseph, a carpenter. One day, much to her great astonishment, the angel Gabriel appeared before her. "Greetings, Mary," the angel said. "Do not be afraid. I bring you the most joyous news. You have been chosen by God to give birth to a son, and you will call him Jesus."

Mary could not even begin to understand the angel Gabriel's words. "How can I give birth to a son," she trembled, "when I am not yet married?"

The angel smiled at Mary. "You will be filled with the Holy Spirit. Your son will be the Son of God. He will be great and his kingdom will last forever. Also, your cousin Elizabeth is going to have a child, even though she is old. You will see that nothing is impossible with God."

Mary bowed her head and rejoiced. When the angel Gabriel had left, she hurried to visit Elizabeth. As soon as Elizabeth heard Mary's news, the baby inside her leaped for joy, and she knew that it, too, was blessed. Mary stayed with her for three months, and soon after she had left, Elizabeth gave birth to a boy and named him John.

"BLESSED ART THOU AMONG WOMEN, AND BLESSED IS THE FRUIT OF THY WOMB."

The Emperor Augustus passed a law that a count be made of every person in the Roman Empire, so people throughout Palestine had to return to their hometowns to be registered. Joseph set off with his young wife, Mary, to his hometown of Bethlehem in Judea.

It was a long, tiring journey from Nazareth to Bethlehem. Mary, who was soon to give birth, traveled on a donkey. When at last they arrived in Bethlehem, they found the town full of people who had also come to be registered.

Luke 1–2
Matthew 1–2

THE BIRTH OF JESUS

WHEN MARY AND JOSEPH arrived in Bethlehem, the streets were crowded, and every inn and lodging was already full. Joseph was anxious to find a room quickly, for he knew that Mary's child would soon be born. At last, Joseph found a place for them to shelter—a cave where a family kept their animals. Meanwhile, wise men in the East began to follow a bright new star they had found in the sky. They were very excited— a new star was the sign that a king had been born.

In the dark and cold of the night, Mary gave birth to the baby Jesus. She wrapped him in strips of cloth and laid him in a manger, where the animals fed. Up in the sky, a star shone brightly to mark the arrival of the Lord.

Out in the fields, shepherds were tending their flocks. Suddenly, an angel appeared. "Do not be afraid," said the angel. "I have news that will bring great joy to you and all mankind. Today, in Bethlehem, a savior has been born who is Christ the Lord. You will find him wrapped in cloths and lying in a manger."

Just then the sky was filled with a host of angels singing their praises to God. The shepherds set off quickly toward Bethlehem where they found the stable, and the baby lying in the manger. They stood in wonder and worshipped the new Messiah.

When the wise men from the East reached Jerusalem, they asked, "Where is the child who has been born King of the Jews?" News of the wise men's search had reached King Herod, who was filled with alarm to hear that a "new king" had been born. His priests had told him about an ancient prophecy that foretold that Christ would be born in the city of Bethlehem.

Herod sent for the wise men. "As soon as you find this new king," he said, "report to me, so that I too may go and worship him." The wise men followed the star, until at last it stopped over the place where Jesus was staying. When they saw him, they bowed down and worshipped him. They presented him with gifts of gold, frankincense, and myrrh.

Then the wise men set off for home, but having been warned in a dream not to go back to Herod, they returned by a different route.

 Matthew 1–2
 Luke 2

THE BOY JESUS

SOON AFTER THE WISE MEN HAD LEFT, an angel of the Lord appeared to Joseph in a dream and warned him to escape immediately to Egypt with Mary and Jesus. "Stay there until I tell you that it is safe," said the angel, "for Herod plans to search the whole of Bethlehem and beyond for the boy and, if he finds him, he will kill him." Joseph knew he had no time to waste, and woke Mary and Jesus from their sleep.

That same night, the family packed their things and set off on the long journey to Egypt.

As soon as Herod realized that he had been outwitted by the wise men, he gave his soldiers orders to kill every boy in Bethlehem under the age of two. He would stop at nothing to protect his kingship.

Some years later, Herod died, and his son took over the throne. Even though Herod had died, Joseph was still too frightened to return to Bethlehem, so he and his family went to live in a town called Nazareth, in Galilee. Every year, Mary and Joseph would travel to Jerusalem for the Feast of Passover. When Jesus was 12, he was allowed to go with them, and for two weeks they joined the celebrations.

When Mary and Joseph finally set off for home with a crowd of friends, they thought Jesus was with them. It was only when they stopped at the end of a day's walking that they discovered he was missing and became frantic with worry.

The worried parents retraced their journey back to Jerusalem, and for two day they searched high and low for Jesus. On the third day, they went to the Temple and found him, surrounded by priests and teachers, asking them questions and listening carefully to their answers.

Mary and Joseph were astonished by what they saw. They called Jesus to them and asked, "Why have you treated us like this? We have been searching for you everywhere." Jesus simply replied, "Surely you knew I would be in my father's house?" Mary and Joseph did not understand what he meant, but they set off back to Nazareth with their son and began to treasure things that happened as signs of Jesus's special relationship with God.

Matthew 2
Luke 2

"... JESUS INCREASED IN WISDOM AND STATURE, AND IN FAVOR WITH GOD AND MAN."

Jesus Is Tested

As a young man, Jesus traveled from Nazareth to the Jordan River to be baptized by John the Baptist. John wandered and preached in the wilderness, preparing the way for Christ. When they met, John felt he was unfit to baptize the Son of God. "I should be baptized by you," he said. But Jesus understood that they were both guided by God's will. He replied, "It is proper for us to do this to fulfill God's wishes." By being baptized, Jesus would be setting an example to his followers.

As soon as Jesus came out of the water, the heavens opened and the Spirit of God in the form of a dove landed on him. A voice from heaven said, "This is my Son, who I love; with him I am well pleased."

After Jesus was baptized, he was led by the Spirit into the desert to be tempted by the Devil. He prayed and fasted for 40 days and 40 nights.

At the end of the 40 days and 40 nights, Jesus was exhausted and hungry. The Devil came to taunt him, saying, "If you are the Son of God, turn these stones into bread." But Jesus refused and said, "The Scriptures say that man does not live on bread alone, but on every word that comes from the mouth of God."

Next, the Devil led Jesus to Jerusalem and up to the highest point of the Temple. "If you are the Son of God," he said, "throw yourself off, for it is written that his angels will save you." But Jesus refused. He would not test the Lord his God.

The Devil then led Jesus to a very high mountain and showed him the kingdoms of the world. "I will give you all of these," he coaxed, "if you will bow down and worship me." But Jesus said, "Away from me, Satan! I will worship the Lord my God, and him only." With these words, the devil disappeared. Angels came down from the sky to tend to Jesus after his ordeal.

Matthew 3–4
Mark 1
Luke 3–4
John 1

"... THOU SHALT WORSHIP THE LORD THY GOD, AND HIM ONLY SHALT THOU SERVE."

Fish and Wine

JESUS RETURNED TO GALILEE and began to spread the word of God. He taught in the synagogues and preached on the hillsides. Very soon, crowds of people began to follow Jesus as he traveled around Galilee. Eventually, he chose 12 of these followers to become his close companions. The first followers of Jesus, known as disciples, were fishermen from Galilee. However, not everybody liked this new teacher. When he taught that God offers salvation to all people, not just the Jews, the people of Nazareth became very angry and drove him out of town.

Peter called for help from another boat, but as soon as it drew close, its own nets were filled, and the boats began to sink. Peter and his companions were astonished, but Jesus simply said, "Don't be afraid; from now on you will catch men."

One morning, Peter, one of Jesus's closest disciples, returned from an unsuccessful night's fishing on the Sea of Galilee. Jesus got into Peter's boat and told him to lower his nets again.

Peter told Jesus that he had been out all night and hadn't caught a thing, but he did as Jesus asked and lowered his nets into the water. In no time at all, the nets were filled with so many fish that the netting threatened to break.

The master of the banquet was pleased and complimented the bridegroom for saving the best wine until last. Jesus had performed the first of many miracles.

Two days later, Jesus was invited to a wedding at Cana in Galilee. Jesus's mother, Mary, was there as well as some of his disciples. Before the celebrations were over, the wine ran out. Mary turned to Jesus for help.

Jesus instructed the servants to fill six huge stone jars with water. He then asked the servants to draw some of the water and to take it to the master of the wedding banquet. Jesus had turned the water into wine, and the master drank it not knowing where the wine had come from.

📖 *Luke 5–6*
John 2

PREACHING AND HEALING

J ESUS SPREAD THE GOOD NEWS throughout Galilee that God's kingdom was arriving among the people. When he wasn't preaching in the synagogues, Jesus spent time teaching his disciples. News of this great teacher traveled fast, and people came from far and wide to listen to him. Many of them were seeking cures from terrible diseases. Jesus healed those with faith and passed on his special message about God.

Jesus told his disciples, "You are the light of the world." Their good behavior and kind deeds would be a shining example for others to follow. They would learn to love their enemies and forgive. The disciples' job would be to show people the true meaning of God's law. Jesus said that they should be humble in their thoughts and actions. They should not seek glory for their good deeds, nor should they be motivated by greed. Only those who applied Jesus's teachings to their daily lives would enter the Kingdom of Heaven.

One day, when Jesus saw crowds gathering to hear him, he went up a mountainside, sat down with his disciples around him, and began to teach God's will to the people. Jesus began his lesson by saying, "Blessed are the poor in spirit, for theirs is the Kingdom of Heaven." He told his disciples that those who put God's will before all else would be rewarded in Heaven. This lesson became known as the Sermon on the Mount.

Jesus offered to go and see the sick man, but the centurion refused, saying, "Lord, you must know that I am not worthy of having you in my house." The centurion was not a Jew and believed that Jesus would not be able to enter his house because of this. The centurion continued, "However, I am used to giving orders and seeing them carried out. If you just say the word, I know my servant will be cured." Jesus, astonished at the centurion's strong faith, told him to go back to his house. Because he had believed in Jesus, his servant had been healed.

Jesus came down from the mountain, followed by crowds of people. A leper approached the group and asked Jesus to heal him. Moved by the leper's plight, Jesus put out his hand and touched the sick man—immediately he was healed.

Jesus preached and traveled around the village of Capernaum for many days. One day, while in the village, a centurion rushed up to Jesus, to tell him that his servant was seriously ill.

📖 *Luke* 6; 11
Matthew 5–8

"AND THEY DID ALL EAT, AND WERE FILLED."

FEEDING THE FIVE THOUSAND

S OON PEOPLE FROM ALL OVER GALILEE traveled to hear what Jesus had to say. The crowds that followed him continued to grow, and many Jews began to believe that Jesus could be the long-awaited Messiah, or "chosen deliverer of Israel." However, as fast as he was becoming popular, Jesus was making enemies as well.

One day, Jesus went by boat to a remote place to spend some time with his disciples. However, he was greeted by crowds of people, eager to hear him preach. When it grew late, the disciples asked him to send the crowds away, for there was nothing for them to eat—they had only five loaves and two fish between them, not enough to feed the crowds.

Instead, Jesus took the disciples' five loaves and two fish, gave thanks to God, and broke the loaves. He gave the food to the disciples and told them to share it out among the people. To their surprise, there was enough to feed every one of the five thousand gathered there.

Jesus sent his disciples back to Galilee by boat. He told the crowds to go home and went up a mountainside alone to pray. A storm began to brew and the disciples' boat, which was now far from land, was rocked by the waves.

Peter got out of the boat and began to walk on the water, but as soon as the wind gusted, he was afraid and began to sink. "Lord save me!" he cried. Jesus held out his hand and caught him, saying, "How little faith you have." His disciples then knew for certain that he was the Son of God, and they worshipped him.

During the early hours of the morning, Jesus walked across the water toward the storm-battered boat. When the disciples saw him, they thought he was a ghost and were terrified. Right away Jesus spoke to them. "Take courage!" he said. "It is I." Peter replied, "If it really is you, Lord, command me to walk across the water to you." "Come," said Jesus.

Matthew 14
Mark 6
Luke 9
John 6

JESUS AND THE PARABLES

J ESUS'S JOURNEY TOOK him next toward Jerusalem. When he traveled through the region of Samaria, he persevered with his teaching, even though it was a region hostile to Jews. Jesus also angered many religious leaders along the way—they did not like him healing on the Sabbath day. However, he continued with his teachings, using stories called parables. Through these stories, Jesus showed people how God's Kingdom should change the way they lived.

O ne day a lawyer asked Jesus how to inherit eternal life. Jesus replied, "You must love your God with all your heart and soul, and you must love your neighbor as yourself." The man asked, "Who do you mean by my neighbor?" To explain, Jesus told him the story of the good Samaritan.

A man was beaten and stripped by robbers and left half dead by the roadside. Soon after, a priest walked along the same road and saw the injured man. He continued on his way on the other side of the road. A little while later, a Levite (a priest's assistant) saw the injured man, and he too hurried on. The two men had believed the injured man was dead, and their religious laws forbade them from touching a dead person.

A Samaritan took the same road, but when he saw the injured man, he took pity on him and tended to his wounds. Then he put the man on his own donkey and carried him to an inn, where he took care of him. The next morning, the Samaritan gave the innkeeper two silver coins and asked him to look after the injured man until he returned. When Jesus had finished the story, he told the expert in law that to be a good neighbor, he must behave as the good Samaritan had and treat everyone as a neighbor, no matter who they were.

The older son was angry that his brother was being treated so well, when he, the eldest, had remained at home loyal to his father. But his father explained, "You are always with me, and everything I have is yours. But we had to celebrate and forgive your brother, because he was lost and now is found."

In the parable of the prodigal son, Jesus described how a father divided his estate equally between his two sons. Shortly afterward, his younger son collected up all his possessions, left home, and went to a distant country. There he lived the life of a prince and squandered all his money on fine clothes, jewels, and entertaining his friends.

The country the son had moved to was soon devastated by famine, and the boy came close to starvation. Eventually, he found work taking care of a farmer's pigs, but he was still hungry most of the time. The son decided to return home, beg forgiveness from his father for abandoning him, and offer to work as his servant.

When his father saw him, he was full of compassion and welcomed him back with open arms. "Father, I no longer deserve to be called your son, make me your servant!" the son cried. But his father would not do this. He ordered soft shoes to be brought for his son's feet and a ring for his finger. He was so pleased his son had returned that he arranged a huge party to celebrate.

Luke 10
Luke 15

ENTRY INTO JERUSALEM

WHEN THEY CAME TO THE REGION of Caesarea Philippi, Jesus asked his disciples who people thought he was. They answered John the Baptist, Elijah, or some other prophet, but Peter confirmed that he knew Jesus to be the Son of God. Jesus then explained to the disciples that he must travel to Jerusalem, where he would suffer, be killed, and rise again. Peter refused to believe it, but six days later, the voice of God came to them from a shining cloud, saying, "This is my own dear Son, with whom I am pleased—listen to him!"

As they neared Jerusalem, Jesus sent two disciples ahead into the next village, where he said they would find a donkey and her colt. "Bring them to me," he said. "Tell anyone who tries to stop you that the Lord needs them." The disciples found the two animals. They brought them back to Jesus and laid their cloaks over the colt for Jesus to sit on.

Thousands of Jews gathered to spread cloaks and branches across the road in front of Jesus. They shouted joyfully, "Hosanna to the Son of David! Blessed is he who comes in the name of the Lord." As Jesus entered Jerusalem, the clamor of the crowds roused the people of the city, who asked, "Who is this?" to which the Jews replied, "This is Jesus, the prophet from Nazareth in Galilee."

When Jesus reached the Temple that he had visited when he was 12, he found it had been turned into a marketplace. Men were selling animals for sacrifice and exchanging money for the festival visitors. This made Jesus very angry. He drove the animals away and scattered the tables covered in money, crying, "How dare you turn my Father's house into a den of thieves!"

Jesus then began to heal the sick who came to see him. The chief priests of Jerusalem watched Jesus's growing popularity with alarm— they were frightened that Jesus was encouraging the people to revolt against their Roman rulers. They became angry when they heard children shouting, "Praise to the Son of David!" The priests asked Jesus, "Do you hear what these children are saying?" Jesus replied, "Yes, I do. Do you want to stop children from praising God?"

▢ *Matthew* 21
Mark 11
Luke 20
John 2; 12

"MY HOUSE SHALL BE CALLED THE HOUSE OF PRAYER."

Jesus Is Arrested

JESUS LEFT THE CITY to stay overnight at the house of a man named Simon, in Bethany. There, a woman poured a jar of expensive perfume over his head. Jesus's disciples were horrified, believing the oil to have been wasted, when it could have been sold for money to feed the poor. However, Jesus told them she was preparing him for burial. By now, Judas Iscariot, one of Jesus's disciples, was beginning to lose his faith in Jesus. He went to the chief priests, who disliked Jesus, and offered to betray Jesus, for a sum of money.

When the Passover festival arrived, Jesus sent his disciples to a house in Jerusalem to prepare for their Passover meal. That evening, during the meal, Jesus announced that one of them would betray him to his enemies. The disciples stared at each other in disbelief and began to ask, one by one, "Surely, Lord, you don't mean me?"

Jesus said, "I will dip my bread into this bowl and give it to the man who will betray me." He did so, and gave the bread to Judas. With a start, Judas left the room. Jesus then gave the disciples bread to eat and wine to drink, saying, "This is my body, which I am giving up for you," and, "This is my blood, which I am shedding for many for the forgiveness of their sins."

Jesus was taken to the house of the High Priest, Caiaphas, where teachers of the law gathered. They tried to find evidence against him but could not find him guilty of any crime. Finally, Caiaphas asked, "Are you the Son of God?" Jesus replied, "I am." The chief priests declared that no man could be the Son of God and that Jesus must be punished for what he had said. The punishment for this would be death.

Peter was sitting outside in the courtyard when a servant of the High Priest said to him, "You were here with Jesus of Galilee." Peter was scared and denied knowing Jesus three times. Then a cock crowed, and Peter remembered that Jesus had told him he would disown him three times before the cock crowed at dawn. Peter wept with shame when he realized what he had done.

📖 *Matthew* 26
   Mark 14
   Luke 22
   John 13; 18

Later, Jesus led his disciples to a garden full of olive trees, called Gethsemane. While the others waited, he walked on further with Peter and the brothers James and John and said to them, "My heart is so full of sorrow that it almost crushes me." Jesus then asked the disciples to keep watch and went off to pray alone. He threw himself to the ground and begged God to spare him.

Jesus went back three times to find his disciples asleep instead of keeping watch, but at last he said, "Sleep no more. Here comes my betrayer." Judas was approaching him, followed by a crowd of men armed with swords. Judas kissed Jesus, and at once Jesus was arrested. The disciples ran away in horror.

"O MY FATHER, IF IT BE POSSIBLE, LET THIS CUP PASS FROM ME …"

THE CRUCIFIXION

EARLY THE NEXT MORNING, the chief priests led Jesus to Pontius Pilate, the Roman Governor. Pilate asked Jesus, "Are you King of the Jews?" to which Jesus replied, "So you say." After that, Jesus refused to say another word, much to Pilate's concern—he knew that the charges against Jesus were false. Pilate made one last effort to help Jesus. At Passover, it was his custom to free a prisoner chosen by the people. Barabbas, a thief, was in jail at that time. Pilate asked the crowd: "Do I release Barabbas, or Jesus who is called Christ?"

The soldiers led Jesus away through the streets of Jerusalem. They had dressed him in purple and had placed a crown made of twisted thorns upon his head. Jesus was made to carry the heavy cross on which he was to be crucified. Crowds of people lined the streets and watched Jesus struggle painfully under the weight of his cross.

While Pilate waited for their reply, his wife told him of a dream whereby she knew that Jesus was innocent of any crime and that they would suffer if they killed him. But the priests and elders whipped up hatred among the crowd, and when Pilate asked them whom they wished to be spared, they all cried, "Barabbas!"

Pilate then asked, "What shall I do with Jesus the Messiah?" and the crowd began shouting at the tops of their voices, "Crucify him! Crucify him!" Pilate saw that a riot might break out. He washed his hands in front of the crowd, saying, "I am not responsible for this man's death. It is your doing." He set Barabbas free as the crowd demanded and handed Jesus over to be crucified.

📖 *Matthew* 27
Mark 15
Luke 23
John 18–19

Jesus was led to a place called Golgotha, where he was crucified. Mary, Jesus's mother, and Mary Magdalene, his friend, watched in sorrow as he was hung upon the cross. Two other men, both criminals, were crucified on either side of him. Below him, soldiers rolled dice to see who would get his clothes. Others hurled insults at him and mocked him. "If you have saved others," they shouted, "then save yourself!"

The sky grew dark as Jesus hung on the cross. Then in the ninth hour, he cried out, "My God, why have you forsaken me?" The curtain in the Temple in Jerusalem ripped in two, and a tremor shook the earth. Jesus said in a loud voice, "Father! In your hands I place my spirit!" and at that moment, he died. A soldier who had watched throughout and seen the strange things that had happened said, "Surely this man was the Son of God!"

As Jesus staggered through the narrow streets of Jerusalem, the soldiers grabbed a man from the crowds. His name was Simon, and he was from the city of Cyrene in North Africa. He was forced to help Jesus carry his heavy burden. Among the crowds that followed them were some women who were weeping. Jesus called to them, "Women of Jerusalem, do not cry for me, cry for yourselves and your children."

"FATHER FORGIVE THEM; FOR THEY KNOW NOT WHAT THEY DO."

THE RESURRECTION

A FEW HOURS AFTER JESUS'S DEATH, a man named Joseph of Arimathea asked Pilate to release Jesus's body to him for burial. Pilate agreed, and Joseph took down the body from the cross. He wrapped it in linen and placed it in a tomb cut out of rock. Then he rolled a stone against the tomb entrance. However, this was not enough for the chief priests and Pharisees. They demanded that the tomb be made secure because of Jesus's promise that he would rise again. The tomb was sealed and soldiers were sent to guard it.

At dawn on the first day after the Sabbath, Mary Magdalene and Mary, mother of James, went to Jesus's tomb to anoint the body with oils. As they arrived, there was a violent earthquake. An angel appeared like lightning and rolled back the stone that blocked the tomb. The guards were so afraid that they fainted.

The angel said to the women, "Do not be afraid. You have come to find Jesus, but he is not here. He has risen, just as he said he would. Come and see the place where he lay, then go and tell the disciples this: He has risen from the dead and is going ahead of you into Galilee. There you will see him."

"FEAR NOT YE: FOR I KNOW THAT YE SEEK JESUS, WHICH WAS CRUCIFIED."

The two women hurried from the tomb to tell the disciples their news. Suddenly, Jesus appeared before them, and they fell to their knees and worshipped him. He said to them, "Do not be afraid, but go and tell my brothers to go to Galilee; there they will see me."

📖 *Matthew 27–28*
Luke 24

The same day, Cleopas and another follower of Jesus were heading for a village called Emmaus. Jesus joined them on the road, but the disciples were unable to recognize him. Jesus asked them what they were discussing and why they looked so sad. "Do you not know what has happened in Jerusalem?" asked one of them. "Jesus of Nazareth, a man powerful in his actions and words before God, has been crucified."

Jesus explained that what had happened in Jerusalem was meant to be and had been foretold in the Old Testament. The disciples' spirits lifted. When they reached Emmaus, they invited Jesus to stay with them. At supper, Jesus took and broke the bread and gave thanks before passing it to them. At once, their eyes were opened and they recognized him, but as they did so, he disappeared.

"JESUS ... SAITH UNTO THEM, PEACE BE UNTO YOU."

"... IT IS THE LORD."

THE ASCENSION

JESUS'S APPEARANCE IN EMMAUS renewed the disciples' faith. When they were next all together, Jesus appeared again. Thomas, one of the disciples, was absent. When he was told what had happened, he said, "Unless I see his wounds, I shall not believe it." A week later, Jesus appeared again and told Thomas to look at the evidence for himself. Thomas looked and said, "My Lord and my God!" Jesus replied, "Because you have seen, you have believed. Blessed are those who have not seen and yet have believed."

The disciples realized then that the man on the shore was Jesus. Peter jumped into the water and swam for the shore. The other disciples followed in the boat, towing the net full of fish. When they landed, they saw a fire with fish cooking over it and some bread. "Bring some of the fish you have caught, and come and have breakfast," Jesus said.

Matthew 28
John 20–21
Acts 1

Jesus appeared to the disciples for a third time by the Sea of Galilee, where they had been fishing without success. In the early hours, Jesus called to them from the shore, though they did not recognize him. "Throw your net on the right side of the boat," he told them. They did so and caught a large number of fish.

When they had finished eating, Jesus asked Peter three times, "Do you truly love me?" After the third time, Peter said, "Lord, you know all things, you know that I love you." Jesus replied, "Feed my sheep." In this way, he signaled to Peter that he had chosen him to be leader of the disciples and the Church.

Jesus then led the disciples to a mountain, where he raised his hands and blessed them. "When the Holy Spirit comes upon you, you will be filled with power," he told them, and he assured them that he would guide them as they took his message out into the world.

His journey at an end, Jesus was lifted up out of the disciples' view, hidden from them in a cloud. As they looked upward, two men in white stood beside them and asked, "Why do you stand here looking at the sky? This Jesus, who has been taken from you into heaven, will come back in the same way you have seen him go into heaven." The disciples understood and returned to Jerusalem to pray and spread the word of the Lord.

"GO ... AND TEACH ALL NATIONS ..."

PEOPLE OF THE BIBLE

DURING HIS TIME ON EARTH, Jesus touched the lives of many people, and on his travels around Galilee, he encountered people from all walks of life. Below are just a few of the people who appear in the New Testament and are featured in the story of this remarkable man named Jesus.

Andrew
Brother of Peter, Andrew was a fisherman from Bethsaida. He was the first disciple to meet Jesus and immediately believed that Jesus was the Messiah. Andrew had first been a disciple of John the Baptist.

Barabbas
A notorious Jewish freedom-fighter, Barabbas was imprisoned for rebellion and murder and was awaiting execution at the time of Jesus's arrest. It was Pontius Pilate's custom to release one Jewish prisoner at Passover. This time, he allowed the crowds to chose who should die—Barabbas or Jesus. The crowds chose Jesus.

Bartholomew
It is possible that Bartholomew, one of the 12 disciples, was the same person as Nathanael, who is mentioned in John's Gospel. Bartholomew passionately believed that Jesus was "the Son of God and King of Israel."

Caiaphas
Appointed by the Romans, Caiaphas was the High Priest and leader of the Jews from 18–36 CE. He presided over Jesus's trial and accused Jesus of blasphemy for claiming to be the Son of God.

Cleopas
A faithful follower of Jesus, Cleopas and a friend were walking from Jerusalem to Emmaus when they met Jesus. He had risen from the dead. They invited Jesus to eat with them and only recognized him when they heard him speak.

David
Jesus is frequently referred to as the Son of David. David was a shepherd when God sent Samuel to anoint him as the future king. David was blessed with God's protection and became Israel's greatest king. The prophets believed him to be the forerunner of the Messiah (Jesus).

Elizabeth
Mary's cousin and wife of Zechariah. Elizabeth had been unable to have a child and was no longer young. However, the archangel Gabriel appeared to Zechariah with the news that Elizabeth would bear a son who would be called John. He became known as John the Baptist.

Gabriel
The archangel Gabriel was one of the highest-ranking angels. He appeared to Mary and to Zechariah with news of the forthcoming births of Jesus and John. Gabriel appears four times in the Bible as a messenger of God.

Herod Antipas
Son of Herod the Great, Herod Antipas ruled in Galilee until 39 CE. He gave his stepdaughter, Salome, the head of John the Baptist and wanted Jesus to perform a miracle for him. Jesus would not be tempted and refused to answer Herod's questions at his trial.

Herod the Great
Ruler of Judea, Galilee, and Samaria between 37 and 4 BCE, Herod the Great's reign was one marked by bloodshed. He was friendly with the Romans, and his fear of a Jewish rebellion led him to destroy potential rivals. He even imagined that members of his own family were plotting to take his throne and had his wife and three of his sons killed.

James
One of the 12 disciples, James was the son of a man called Alphaeus. Little else is known about James.

James, son of Zebedee
A disciple of Jesus, James was the brother of John. Like Peter, James was a fisherman on the Sea of Galilee. They, together with John, were with Jesus at a number of significant events during his ministry. James was considered to be one of Jesus's closest companions.

John
Believed to be the younger brother of James, son of Zebedee. Jesus nicknamed James and John "Sons of Thunder" because of their fiery tempers. John is referred to as the disciple "whom Jesus loves" and may be the author of John's Gospel.

John the Baptist
Son of Elizabeth and Zechariah, John's holy mission was to prepare the way for Jesus. He was a prophet who preached in the Judean desert and baptized people in the Jordan River to wash away their sins. John the Baptist was beheaded by Herod Antipas on the request of Herod's stepdaughter, Salome.

Joseph
Husband of the mother of Jesus, Mary, Joseph was a descendant of David. He lived in Nazareth and worked as a carpenter. Soon

after Jesus's birth, an angel warned Joseph of Herod the Great's plan to kill the baby Jesus. Joseph took his family to Egypt for safety, returning to Nazareth only after Herod's death.

Joseph of Arimathea

A wealthy and influential Jew, Joseph was a secret follower of Jesus. When Jesus was crucified, Joseph asked Pontius Pilate to release his body to him. He wrapped the body in clean cloth, then buried Jesus in a tomb cut out of rock. He sealed the tomb by rolling a large boulder across the entrance.

Judas Iscariot

The only disciple not from Galilee, Judas came from Kerioth in South Judea. He is always mentioned last in the list of disciples in the Bible. Judas betrayed Jesus to the Jewish authorities by leading them to him in the Garden of Gethsemane and identifying him with a kiss. Judas was paid 30 silver coins to betray Jesus but later returned the money and hung himself in remorse.

Mary

Pledged to marry Joseph, the virgin Mary was visited by the archangel Gabriel with the news that she would be the mother of the Son of God. She traveled with Joseph from her home in Nazareth to give birth to Jesus in Bethlehem. During his ministry, Mary became a disciple of Jesus.

Mary Magdalene

A devoted follower of Jesus, Mary Magdalene traveled with Jesus and cared for his needs. She stood grief-stricken by his cross as he died and was one of the first to meet him when he rose again. After finding his tomb empty, Mary Magdalene saw Jesus but did not recognize him until he spoke her name.

Matthew

A tax collector for Roman ruler Herod Antipas, Matthew may also have been called Levi. Like all tax collectors, Matthew would have been despised by the Jews for collecting money for the Romans. He was so attracted by Jesus's teachings that he gave up his job to follow him. It is thought that Matthew was another Gospel author.

Peter

Also known as Simon Peter, the fisherman Peter was the brother of another disciple, Andrew. He was one of the first disciples chosen by Jesus, who changed his name to Peter when he acknowledged Jesus as the Messiah. Peter was the leader of the inner circle of three apostles—Peter, John, and James—and became the leader of the 12. Although he denied knowing Jesus three times prior to the Crucifixion, Jesus met with him after the Resurrection to restore his love.

Philip

A disciple of Jesus, Philip came from the town of Bethsaida, along with Peter and Andrew. He had no doubt right from the beginning that Jesus was the Messiah.

Pontius Pilate

The governor of Judea under the Roman Emperor Caesar from 26–36 CE. Jesus was brought in front of Pilate for judgment after his trial by the Jewish elders.

Simon of Cyrene

A Jew from Cyrene in Africa, Simon was visiting Jerusalem during the festival of Passover, at the time of Jesus's trial. As he stood with the crowds watching Jesus stumble under the weight of the wooden cross, Roman soldiers ordered Simon to help Jesus carry the cross.

Simon the Zealot

The Zealots were a group of freedom-fighters who despised the Romans and challenged their rule. Simon was believed to be one of them. When he became a disciple, he lived alongside Matthew, someone he would previously have hated as a traitor because of his work as a tax collector for the Romans who ruled the area.

Thaddaeus

Also known as Judas, son of James, it is possible that Thaddaeus changed his name so as not to be confused with Judas Iscariot after the latter's treachery.

Thomas

A disciple of Jesus, Thomas was also known as Didymus (meaning "twin"). He was not with the other disciples when they first saw Jesus risen from the dead and refused to believe it until he could feel the Lord's wounds for himself. Shortly afterward, Jesus appeared to Thomas and rebuked him for his lack of faith. It was this incident that earned him the nickname "Doubting Thomas."

"HIS BLOOD BE ON US, AND ON OUR CHILDREN."

INDEX